T0063666

THIS EDITION
Editorial Management by Oriel Square
Produced for DK by WonderLab Group LLC
Jennifer Emmett, Erica Green, Kate Hale, *Founders*

Editors Grace Hill Smith, Libby Romero, Maya Myers, Michaela Weglinski;
Photography Editors Kelley Miller, Annette Kiesow, Nicole DiMella;
Managing Editor Rachel Houghton; **Designers** Project Design Company;
Researcher Michelle Harris; **Copy Editor** Lori Merritt; **Indexer** Connie Binder;
Proofreader Larry Shea; **Reading Specialist** Dr. Jennifer Albro; **Curriculum Specialist** Elaine Larson

Published in the United States by DK Publishing
1745 Broadway, 20th Floor, New York, NY 10019

Copyright © 2023 Dorling Kindersley Limited
DK, a Division of Penguin Random House LLC
23 24 25 26 10 9 8 7 6 5 4 3 2 1
001-334128-Sept/2023

A catalog record for this book
is available from the Library of Congress.
HC ISBN: 978-0-7440-7578-6
PB ISBN: 978-0-7440-7581-6

DK books are available at special discounts when purchased in bulk for sales promotions, premiums,
fundraising, or educational use. For details, contact: DK Publishing Special Markets,
1745 Broadway, 20th Floor, New York, NY 10019
SpecialSales@dk.com

Printed and bound in China

The publisher would like to thank the following for their kind permission to reproduce their images:
a=above; c=center; b=below; l=left; r=right; t=top; b/g=background

Alamy Stock Photo: agefotostock / Marevision 30cla, Nature Picture Library / Shane Gross 1cb, 6-7, 28-29, 30cl,
Andre Seale / VWPics 26-27, WaterFrame_mus 27br; **Dreamstime.com:** Greg Amptman 25crb,
Fiona Ayerst / Fionaayerst 12-13, 30tl, Thomas Lenne 4-5, Phillip Lowe 21br, Seadam 16bl;
Getty Images: Corbis Documentary / Clouds Hill Imaging Ltd. 14cl, 30bl, Image Source / Ken Kiefer 2 16-17, 24-25;
naturepl.com: Graham Eaton 3cb, Shane Gross 8-9, 10-11, 14-15, 22-23;
Shutterstock.com: Anita Kainrath 18-19, 20-21, 30clb

Cover images: *Front:* **Dreamstime.com:** Punnawich Limparungpatanakij b, VetraKori;
Back: **Dreamstime.com:** Kareemov1000 clb, Lidiia Lykova cra

All other images © Dorling Kindersley
For more information see: www.dkimages.com

For the curious
www.dk.com

LIFE OF A
Baby Lemon Shark

Ruth A. Musgrave

Contents

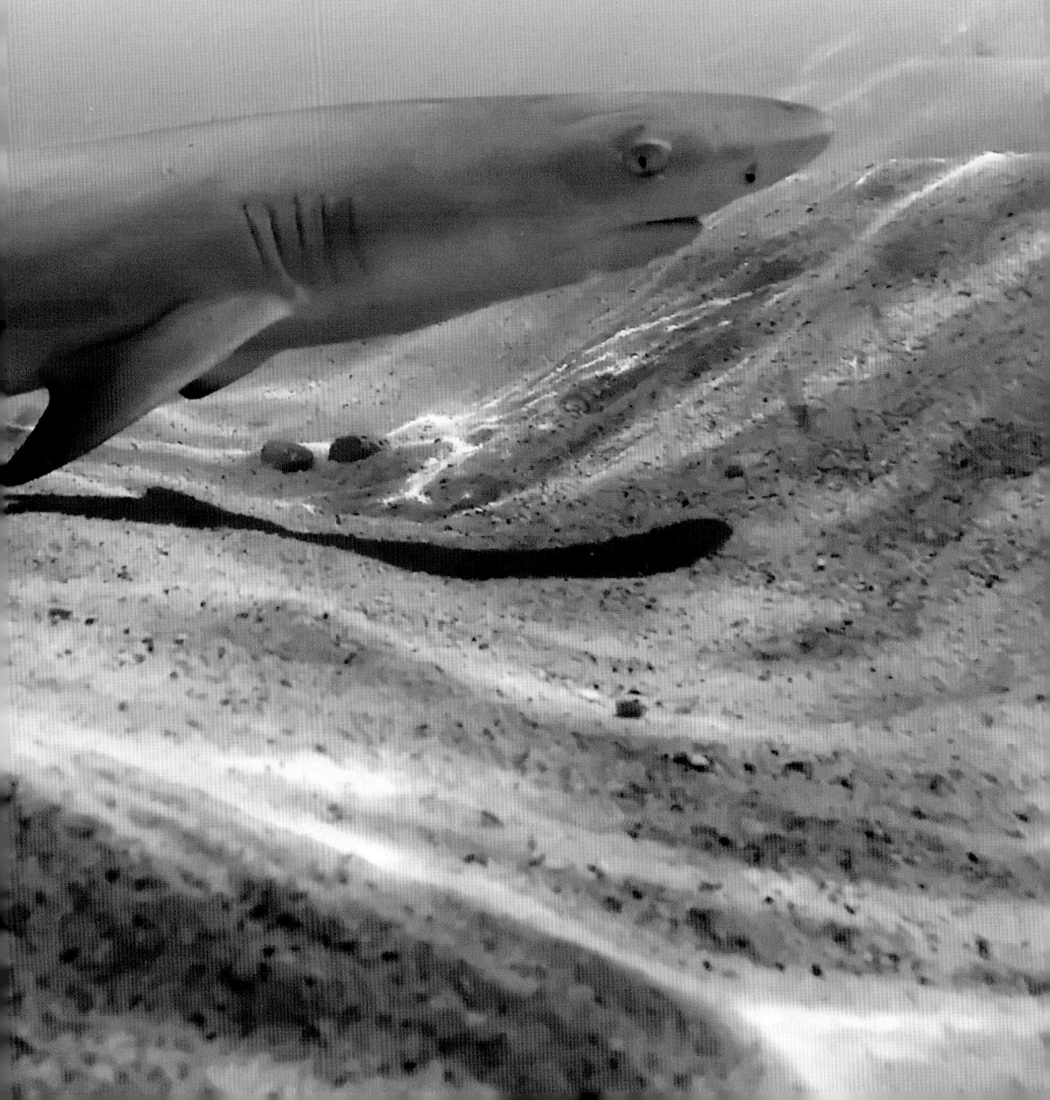

Hiding in the Roots

The baby lemon shark
swims alone
near the shore.
It lives where the
water is warm.

mangrove
trees

Trees grow in the sea here, too. The roots make a safe place for the shark to grow up.

The newborn pup
is very small.
But it already knows
a lot of things.
It knows how to swim
and find food.

The baby shark also knows how to hide from hungry animals.

Big Breath of Water

Like all sharks, the baby shark is a fish. Fish breathe with their gills.

The water flows
into their mouth.
Then, it washes over their
gills so that the fish
can breathe.

gills

Fine Fins

Swish. Swish. The pup moves its tail from side to side.
Its tail helps it swim fast to catch dinner or to get away from danger.

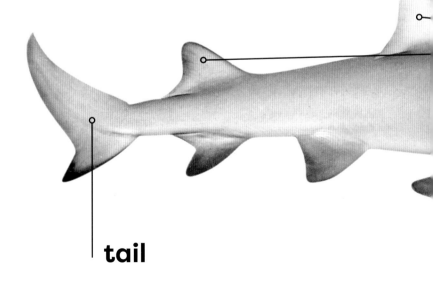

tail

The baby shark uses its two front fins to turn and stop.
The fins on its back and belly help, too.
They keep the shark from tipping over while it swims and turns.

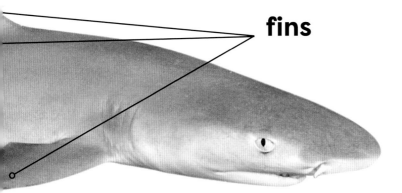

fins

Super Scales

Scales cover its body.
Scales are tough
and sharp.
They protect the baby's
skin from sand and rocks.

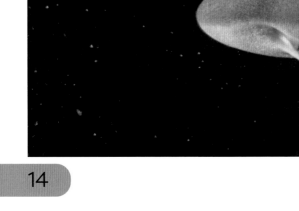

scales

The baby lemon shark's color helps protect it, too. The yellowish color blends in with the sand. That makes the baby shark harder to see. Then, it can hide from bigger animals.

Quiet Hunter

The baby swims between the tree roots.
It is hunting for food.
It swims quietly.

roots

It uses its senses.
It looks for something
to eat.

eye

The pup is a good listener.
It listens for noisy animals.

ear

The baby shark swims
toward a sound.

The baby shark also uses its nose to find food. The water carries the scent of fish and shrimp.

nostrils

The pup smells
a yummy fish.
The baby shark
swims toward it.

The smell grows stronger
and stronger.
The pup swims closer
and closer.

Baby shark opens its mouth wide.
Oh no! It misses!
The fish gets away.

Shrimp for Dinner

The baby shark
tries again.
It looks, listens,
and smells.
This time it finds
a shrimp.

The pup grabs the shrimp with its rows of sharp teeth. It does not chew its food. The baby shark swallows the shrimp in one gulp!

teeth

Bigger and Farther

The baby shark
will grow bigger.
It will eat bigger
and faster animals.

The baby shark will swim farther from this safe place. It will explore more of the sea as it grows.

But near the shore is the perfect place to swim right now.
Swim on, baby shark!

Glossary

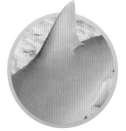

fins
body parts that help
a shark swim and turn

gills
body parts that help
a fish breathe

mangrove trees
trees that grow in
shallow ocean water

nostrils
body parts that help
a fish smell

scales
small, hard plates that
cover a fish's skin to
protect it

Index

Quiz

Answer the questions to see what you have learned. Check your answers with an adult.

1. Where do baby lemon sharks hide?

2. How do sharks breathe?

3. Which body parts does a lemon shark use to turn?

4. Name two things lemon sharks eat.

5. True or False: Baby lemon sharks chew their food.

1. Near the shore in tree roots 2. They use their gills 3. Fins
4. Shrimp and fish 5. False